Last Steps of Christopher

Carmen Kleinwachter

Published by Daniel Wetta Publishing
Copyright 2017 Carmen Kleinwachter

For more information, please visit the author page:

www.danielwetta.com/carmenkleinwachter

Dedication

These poems were written in memory of my son, Christopher Kenneth Kleinwachter, who died in service of our country. He passed away on November 29, 2006. His loving mother, Carmen Kleinwachter, is the author of this book and hopes it heals and helps others in the process of dealing with a loved one's death.

Listing of Poems

Dreams that are Real

It has been said in the Bible that dreams would happen, and my son was a recipient of a prophetic dream. When he was living at home with me, he came out of the bedroom and told me that he had a dream and it represented war. I believe he was being told that our country would be at war. I dismissed this and went about my day.

About two weeks later, he came to me again. Only this time, he told me that the family was in the mountains and that Jesus came. I was excited to hear this, as the divorce had divided our family badly. To think that we would be together in one place was exciting.

But I never thought about these dreams until after Christopher's death.

After 9/11, things started to happen. Chris and I talked, and he assured me the National Guard would not be sent to the war in the Mid-East.

However, not long after that conversation, he called to tell me that he wanted me to come where he was living, as he needed to talk with me. As we walked the trail, he told me that he was going to be sent to Afghanistan. We were at war. Just as the dream had declared.

Then, on November 29, the second dream was fulfilled. Jesus did come to get Chris in the mountains like he had told me. Only these were the Afghanistan mountains, and his family there was the military one.

I also had a dream that Chris came to me and put his uniform away.

And so, he did.

But his retirement from service came when he was thrown from the gunning position onto the ground.

My Son

My son, I stand beside you, so very near.
Is that in your eyes a tear?
You seem so brave as you walk away.
Just another mission we are on today.

When I called, I asked so sincerely
They won't send you, my dear?
Oh!
No?

Mom, not the National Guard!
That question seems so hard.
We will never leave here.

And yet, they did send my dear son
Who used to play solider at ten.
Now he looks so very handsome in the end,
Looking asleep.

No, my mother, but the flag you keep.
Shut the lid, put me in the ground.

Twenty-one-gun salute is the only sound.

'Twas the Night Before Deployment

'Twas the night before deployment
And all through the house
No one was happy,
Not even the mouse.

For soon a soldier much loved
Would sadly disappear
Protecting our country
He held so dear.

Others in country were nestled in bed
Not a clue for all the goodbyes to be said.
Then what to my wondering eyes should appear?

A military plane to take my loved one so dear!

The soldier ascended the steps one by one
Wondering how soon this venture would be done.
My soldier was not alone on that flight.
The sky seemed so big as it went out of sight.

The faces of comrades all looked the same
Not one of them wanted to mention the strain.
This thing called liberty and freedom to us
A feeling to them a must to defend.
Disembarking to a country not known
The true walk of the patriot was shown.
So, to all the soldiers I do salute
In military uniforms worn like a suit.

Thank you again and again.
I will pray for you until the end
And that all times which we call war
Are closed forever and there are no more.

God bless you, my friend,
Whom I don't even know
'Till we meet somewhere
In heaven or here below.

Guidance Prayer

Dear Lord,

Be with the soldiers tonight.
Protect and guide them by your light.
Keep them safe and keep them keen
To the enemy's attack that can't be seen.
Help them carry the banner high
Which they are protecting with their lives.

Freedom's cost is very high, and you are the one
Who paid the highest price.
Father, can we ever stop and see
That you are the one whom we must seek?
We have become lazy and take for granted
So many blessings along our way.

Help me to become a mighty warrior for you.
To love and keep what is true.
Jesus, you are my best friend.
Help me to see what you want me to do.
I can do it with you at my side
To direct and guide me all the while.

Amen

America

America means love.
We have the right to love each other in peace and
harmony.

A is for Almighty God, who created each of us for our own
special way.
M is for the men and women who have served to keep us
free.
E is for everyone in everyplace where equality thrives in
the ideal of "America."
R is for the color of blood shed to protect the right to
liberty.
I is for individuality and freedom to pursue dreams that
God places in our hearts.

C is for the calling that God gives us to join hands and work to uphold our nation.
A is for the American ideal to be the land of the free, the brave and the loving.

This special nation which God has given to us:
Do we honor His gift and keep it free for all?

National Guard

N Nation.
A Attention.
T Time and talent.
I Individual.
O Obedience.
N Natural.
A Assembled as one.
L Loyal.

G Guardian.
U United.
A Action.
R Readiness.
D Direction.

Army Prayer

Arm me, oh Lord, for what you are calling me to do. Let me rest on your arm of favor and protection, oh God.

Arm me, oh Lord, from the fiery darts of the enemy, using weapons of love, joy and peace.

Instruct me, oh Lord, in the strategy of warfare in which to win this battle of life.

Help me face the enemy of my soul with the force of singing praises
Celebrating the high standards of you.

Remind me, oh Lord, not to fall prey to needless murmuring and complaining.
May the drill sergeant only drill out the things not pleasing and fitting to you.

May the armor we wear daily bear the likeness of you.

Praise and honor are yours, Lord, forever and ever.
Help us to march to the beat of your heart
And to proclaim the high calling that you have for each of us.

We ask this in Jesus' name, the one and only son of God, son of man.

Amen

Leave No Man Behind

Leave no man behind: We must believe and pursue this. We must unite and conquer those who take from us. We must get back what has been given to us and which we allowed to be stolen from our hands. Our hands look empty, but they are full of weapons of praise for the one who made us in His image. We must join our hands with our brothers and sisters. God loves us unconditionally and has taught us the power of forgiveness. We must have confidence in His arms and weaponry of love.

Our attitude should be one of victory, for Christ paid the ultimate price and reserved us a place in eternity with Him. He, through His obedience, reclaimed mankind to be near and dear to the Trinity. The Alpha and Omega has numbered our days in which we are to believe that the time is near and dear to Him.
The angels rejoice in excitement as we honor and praise Him with our lives and bring numbered people to Him. God has made divine appointments for us to receive others

into the family of integrity and pureness of His love. We must remember to have the attitude of gratitude for the victory He has won for us. He offers a place with Him in eternity - a noble and precious nearness to Him.

His call is to leave no man behind! Therefore, acclaim the majesty of the great I AM! He has offered us a divine appointment to love Him for eternity.

Our efforts for Him are not small tasks, but with Him all things are possible.

LEAVE NO MAN BEHIND

Love
Everyone
Acclaim
Victory
Eternity

Nobility
Obedience

Mankind
Attitude
Numbers

Believe
Excitement
Honor
Integrity
Nearness
Divine

Army of One Prayer

We come to you, dear Lord, asking you to help us to become an Army of One in you.

Help us to be united and fight not against each other, but against the enemy of our soul.

Help us to cover each other's back and confront the enemy head-on together.

Teach each of us to take our appropriate position in the battle of life.

Help us capture our enemies with love and understanding, knowing that we, too, were once the enemy.

Help us to aim our sights on things above worldly desires.

Help us march to the sound of praise and adoration to our Lord and King.

Help us to drill and stay in communication with our High Commander-in-Chief so that we defend the territory He has told us to defend and conquer and establish new territories each day.

Help us pursue what seems impossible to us for Him.

Help us put one foot in front of the other day by day and march to your tune and calling.

You are within our reach through prayer and obedience.

Thank you, Lord, for your leadership.

In Jesus' precious name, we ask these petitions.

Amen.

These Boots

These boots were made for marching,
And that is what they do.
They march to the tune of obedience
When drill sergeant yells what to do.

We march together in battle
Watching each other's back
Wondcring, but always ready,
Alert for the enemy's attack.

Not one of us is eager
To have to stand alone.
That's why we are called one.
No division is ever shown.

We don't shine our shoes to be pretty
Instead, we take delight
In putting our best foot forward
In the disciplined army fight.

We are brothers and sisters in each and every way:
Our family military National Guard, 188th, to stay.

Some Say

Some say that I am unfit to do the job at hand.
But you have me there and still encourage me to go
forward
In this valley of the shadow of death.
I see death all around me.

Rumors here and there.
Things said that make we wonder if I will ever get out of
this valley alive.
I look up and see the tremendous heights before me.
I wish I were on the mountain tops.
I realize that I have no way to climb there now.
I only have the option to pursue the rocks and obstacles
that are in my way.
One by one.

Look ahead and do not look behind.
The way is very narrow and hard now.

It is the narrow way that leads to heaven, not the broad
way.
The rocks are jagged.
They cut into my flesh,
Leaving my wounds exposed to the elements
And the blood rushes out
To cleanse the severances of my life.

Help me to continue my journey, Lord
With Thee.

Battle Stress

He picked up his rifle and headed towards the line.
His eyes were fixed, and he could discern
That there was something moving out there!

Oh! His heart beat faster and faster as he approached.
He could feel it up in his throat.
He swallowed hard; he thought someone might hear.

He would not allow anyone to know he felt fear.
Then all of a sudden it sprung with a leap
It had not two but four big feet.

He jumped straight up in the air.
It was a rabbit with no hair.
Hare today, gone tomorrow, the soldier sighed.

Why Not Love?

Speaking of hatred, why not love?
We hate another but someone is in love
With that enemy we are trying to destroy.

We call it victory when a battle is won,
But is it really a victory when someone lost a son
Or perhaps a daughter?

We judge and objectify our enemy and draw lines
That define him. We think we know who we are
And what we stand for.

Always there is someone who is in harm's way.
They left to go to work or play today.
Maybe it is their last day.

We carry our own messages, that is true.

I carry mine. What about you?
Hate feels heavy; love feels light:
It's legacy a field of victors.

The Bridge

I may not be someone you know.
I may not seem to even care.
But remember where I have been,
And you haven't been there.

I have fought for freedom with my life.
You were always on my mind.
Thinking about home all the time,
Wishing this thing we call war was all behind.

"Take a bullet for me.
Please keep safe my liberty."
Then I come home to find
Someone thought it was not worth their time.

Wish they could have been with me.
Fighting for their freedom, you see
It isn't easy as you think.
Come with me and bridge our link.

Another

Looking – aiming – thinking – weighing
The thought of another, called
Enemy.
Making the mark clean and sharp his sight.
He aims at the E n e m y and hears his heart
Pump.
He must remember: it is either him or me
The P u m p must be quieted for a moment in
Time.
He pulls the trigger and knows the bullet will fly
Through T i m e, and someone somewhere will be
Hit.
He hears thunderous rain of bullets roar
Missing and dodging, not 100 percent sure the H i t
Lodged
He makes his way carefully to the enemy line.
Seeing the bulled L o d g e d into a person called
Mankind,
He looks at the face of that dead on the ground.
Knowing that one more M a n k i n d is
No more
When, oh when will another enemy pump time to
Lodge into mankind a bullet of hatred no more?
We justify our thoughts of another
When we should just look into his living eyes.

Walk in Unity

When we are being tempted, it is a like a drill sergeant yelling at us.
All sorts of negative remarks about us to break us down.
Stupid, no good.
Don't know what you are doing.
Then if we fall prey, we lose our step.
We are out of line and no longer in the uniform motion of our fellow soldiers.
May we all come in agreement and walk in unity?
That we can become one in Him,
As He is one with the Father and Holy Spirit.

Humility. Simplicity. Unity.

Oh, Soldier

Oh, soldier, can you see
What you have done for me?

You've preserved my very life,
My enjoyment of liberty.

Can we really stand alone?
Togetherness you soldiers have shown.

May we ever salute you
In the red, white, and blue!

May the flag that we see
A reminder to us be.

That your life has kept us free.
Ever grateful we should be.

Oh, soldier we don't deserve what you do for us.
You defend others, and not a word -do we hear

Of the injustices of some you defend.
You do what you believe is right
While others quietly do nothing.

Dream Gift

As I lay upon my bed,
My pillow, my friend it has been said.
Thinking and planning the day.
Falling asleep...what can I say?

What to my wondering dreams appear
But me in a crowd, oh dear!
Then, oh so far away, I see
Somebody near and dear to me.

But, alas! I know you're no more!
Yet, through the crowd you soar,
Not pushing or shoving but coming near.
Is that my Christopher, my son, so dear?

I look at him, and there's not a word.
He gives me a gift as he comes forward.
Handing it to me, my delight!
It is royal blue, just right!

As I held the gift I had been given
I realized that he had been living
In my dream, just to come around
To bestow the gift he had found.

What is the meaning of this to me?
Is it special for everyone to see?
He gave up his life for you and me.
Love is amazing, it sets you free!

Four Brave Men Died from the 188th

Four brave men went off to war,
Proudly wearing the uniforms that they were told to wear.
They got to know each other well as brothers.
Because of their fellow soldiers, they were one.
Then one day to deep dismay two were taken.
Such sorrow, such shock.
But war is what it is and so:
March on as one.
Then just when all seemed right, another was taken.
Just when the tears quieted still, alas, it happened so
quickly.
One more was taken from the 188th.

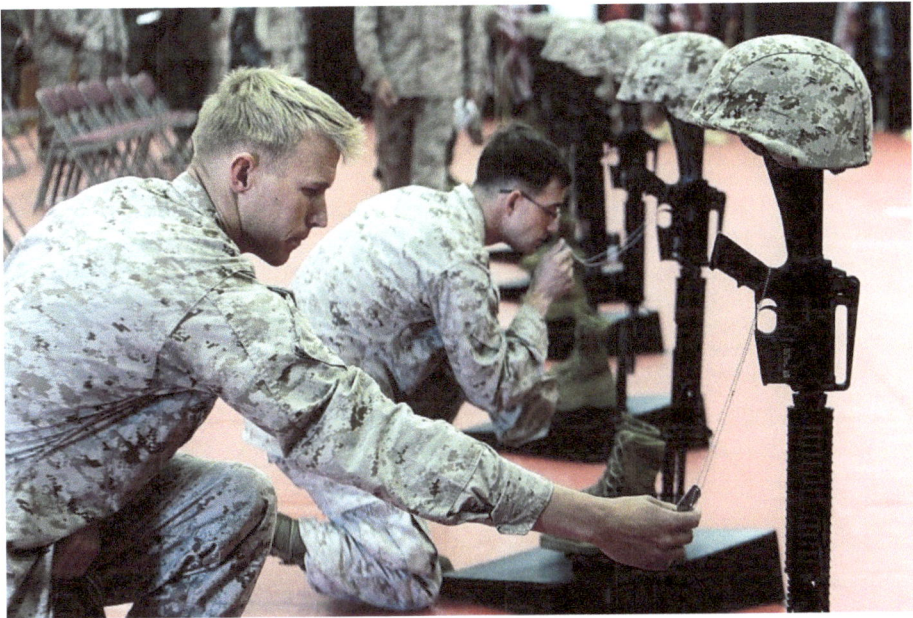

My Gold Star Mom

She may not have been anyone special
But she was to me.

She did many wondrous things
That others did not see.

She held my hand when we went for walks.
She cried with me on our many talks.

She put her hand in my hand
When I needed an added friend.

She understood me when you did not understand.
She accepted me just as I am.

She never pretended to be perfect.
Her imperfections were clear to see.

These may have mattered to you
But not to me.

My mom is a Gold Star mom
Because she loved me unconditionally.

Yellow Ribbon

"Tie a yellow ribbon around the tree."
To me it should be purple or blue!
Fighting to protect and serve is never the color of fear.
It takes a lot to fight the good fight
and wrap yourself in the armor you need to defend
what you believe is the right thing to do.
So why yellow? My ribbons are true blue.

Garfunkel

I had a cat named Garfunkel
He really liked to sing
He wasn't always the best
That really wasn't his thing.
He stayed in the house with me
Which wasn't exactly what he wanted
But that is what was to be.
Living so comfortably
Like every other night, I headed for bed.
He inside with me is the way it was led.
He watched me as I turned off the lights,
Ready to sleep, tucked in bed so tight.
About the time my snoring began, his awful music he sang,
Meowing up and down the floor.
Me wishing, "NO MORE!"
He paced and meowed all the night, in the dark, out of sight.
All night long his song of woe.
But then I didn't know
About the time his final song was sung.
I heard a noise and felt undone.
It was a heavy knock on the door.
Wondering, yet knowing what it was for.
Two men in sad uniform, wearing the face of grim forlorn,
Delivering some news for me,
Not a thing I wanted to see.
The look of concern on their face
Was a wish to be some other place.
These words they had to say:
"Chris died yesterday.

He atop a Humvee rode.
Tumbled over, we were told.
He hit his head upon the ground
And never another word to sound."
So, they said a prayer for me.
I looked, but Garfunkel I could not see.
He knew the message had arrived:
Chris is no longer alive.

Beautiful Feet

How beautiful are your feet?
For they marched and defended my right of life, liberty,
and the pursuit of happiness.

How beautiful are your hands?
They held the weapons to fight for my right to live in the
country I have chosen to make home.

How beautiful are your eyes?
They watched and saw and directed the things needed to
be done to protect, honor and serve.

How beautiful are you?
For you took a vow and kept your word and put yourself in
harm's way for me.

How beautiful are my words?
When I say to you, "Thank you."
They may not be all the words you would like to hear,
But it is all I know what to say.
There are only one other's hands, feet, and eyes that are
more beautiful,
Those of our true commander-in-chief.

He is the one who spoke the very essence of life for you
and me,
And then He allowed His feet and hands to be burrowed
with holes
Proving that His love is so immense, so complete that He
could not hold it all.
So, He allowed His life to be committed to saving all of us,

As you gave your life and sacrificed yourself for the country you love.

He sacrificed for all in hope we would see how much He loves you and me.
Isaac carried the wood for a sacrifice and was spared his loss.
Jesus carried the cross and spared you and me.
What words can I say but, "Thank you?"
Not only to Jesus, but to you, for what you have done for me.

Will I survive?

Knocking and seeing no light,
Waiting and seeing the look of fright.

Yes, the message was true.
Your child died for the red, white, and blue.

Kneeling on bended knee,
Praying, saying words, could it be?

Telling me that my son
Was the one.

Who died today,
In Afghanistan miles away.

Soon they left my side.
Tears were in my eyes.

Now as the miles I drive, I wonder:
Will I survive?

They put my son into the ground.
Peace, can it be found?

The one who gave him to me
Now has him in eternity.

Comfort

They said God will comfort me.
How these words ring so true!
His words kept me free
When Chris died for the red, white and blue.

From the moment I heard the news,
He sent me a special friend
So that I would not lose
Two songs that never end:
"Peace Like a River" and "Be Still My Soul"
Kept me in peace, this I know.

Running continually in my head,
The songs let me rest, it was said.
People praying for me daily
(This is not a maybe.).
Others' hearts were breaking
In the hour of sorrow partaking.
People coming from far and near,
Some weeping, some in fear.
For another soldier had been found,
Just a week earlier from another town.
He died in service for us to be free.
Dying for the keep of liberty.
So, this army united in one
Had lost a total of four lovely sons.

Thank you, Lord, for your comfort to me.
You are a lovely savior to set me free.
From such terrible sorrow that could have no end.
Jesus, you're not just my Savior. You're my friend.

The Forgiving

The words about the death of my son were enough.
But wait, there was a mistake!
The papers said that it was under investigation.
How could this be?
He was dead as dead could be.
How can you investigate, interrogate someone who is
dead?
But that is what the papers read.
Do you want to know the story?
Do you want the truth?
Someone misunderstood the orders,
And then it happened so quick.
The Humvee rolled over and then it was done.
The one that was living
Will no longer see another sun.

So, in a weird sense of way,
The Lord answered my prayer that I did say.
I had asked for a change of heart.
Let it beat for someone's forgiveness.
But, Lord, you must do it your way.

My son's death was the only way, they say.

The Lord sees farther than we can intend.
He prepares a table for enemies, not friends.
Sitting across the table,
What in her face did I seek?
The letter she had seen,
But now the writer did meet.

I heard from a soldier that someone was the one.
But now seeing the other, victory would be won.
Forgiveness for another is freeing to thee.
It is wonderful for you, but much better for me,
To settle a matter or to settle the score.
To hold hatred is never a reward.
To see the light of day
In a brand-new way.
Forgiveness wins the battle.
The Lord will repay.

The Patriot Guard

The Patriot Guard came to help us defend the right to a proper funeral without any disruption from outside pressures.

Patriot Guard

P is for patriot and our prayers for you.
A is for attitude and our appreciation.
T is for the time and travel you have put on those bikes.
R is for readiness to ride again for righteousness and the right to grieve in peace.
I is for the invitation to shield the mourning for incredible ability to stand guard.
O is for the orchestration of patriotism and for the opportunities to find solace.
T is for the thankfulness we have for your thoughtfulness.

G is for all the goodness you share with others.
U is for all your understanding.
A is for all the avenues of protection that you open.
R is for all the roads that you have traveled in your mission.
D is for your dedication to your cause.

His foot hit the kick stand and he rode away.
He felt his heart thumping as he rode into the eastern sky.
One more body, one more memory to put to rest.
It was not complete and it was put to the test.
There were those ready to fight
To protest a funeral with all their might.
One more time he would take a stand to watch

The loved ones walk by that tearful spot.
They call it a funeral, and that is to be the end.
It can send shivers up your spine when the witness it does send.
How can these people who say they are standing for what is right
Try and catch the tears of the grieving and say it is right?
To protest a tear that falls on the cheek and say that what they are doing is complete!
When someone is in sorrow, and it is plain to see,
You don't need more misery, you need company.
These people who swear that what they are doing is right:
When they are in the coffin, will we have the right
To protest their protesting, or will we be met
With a sorrowful eye of regret?
Pointing a finger, only stand to say
There are fingers pointing the other way!
Who will stand by their side when their time does come?
Will we hear a "kick stand" and another run?
Putting all my feelings aside,
You came to my rescue when all I wanted was to lie down and die.
Putting my feelings first,
You gave me a tissue to dry my tears.
Yet all the while your heart was ready to burst.
Not letting me see how you felt,
You walked with me through those hard and difficult times,
Never complaining-always remaining close by my side.
Unwilling to see a stranger left alone,
You came to be with me, not knowing how I would respond,

Never questioning how or when the dammed-up feelings
would break loose.
You just sat quietly, listening, despite your own heart ache.
Many a time you may have wanted to fly away and never
come back.
You got on your bike yet another time.
You rode those many miles of memories,
Wanting to protect and, all the while, never looking back.
You call yourself a Patriot Guard.
My, what a name!
I could call you a lot of good things, but that name
remains.
Your tears you hold back until the time has come.
Yet one more journey gone with the setting sun.

The Final Ground

A man-stranger came to my side
To comfort me.
He walked by my side after the others had fled.
He dried my tears as he was led.
He protected and defended me,
Keeping me safe perfectly.
He is called a casualty officer.
He was standing in for Chris.
My son never made it home.
The man made sure that I was not alone.
As we traveled to Chris' final ground,
Twenty-one- gun salute was the sound, then

SILENCE.

In Memoriam: Corporal Christopher Kleinwachter

21-Gun-Salute

When my son died, I was honored. What did I do?
Absolutely nothing. People blessed me, encouraged me,
but why? I did nothing.

As I went out for a walk, I thought about that day. Then I
thought about Christ.

When we die to ourselves, we put our past in the coffin
and bury it. It is to be put to rest and not to be seen or
looked at again. Sitting in the pew, I remember this. Dying
to ourselves is exactly that to God.

Our trespasses, phew! We stink when we come to Him in
ourselves. We are nothing in ourselves.

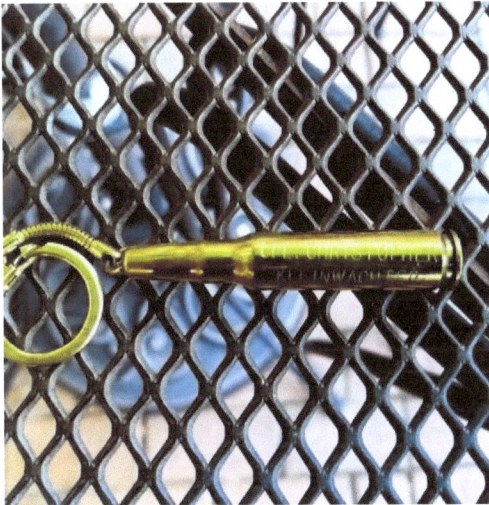

I thought, how did I
deserve all of this?
People came to honor
my son, but in the
process, I was the one
receiving what he
deserved. Then I
thought about Christ
and how He died for us
and how we get so
much through what He
did for us. When others
come to us, hopefully, they will see Christ in us so they
can be blessed. We are accepted and honored by God just
because of what Christ did. We did absolutely nothing.
Nothing did we do to deserve the honor to be called a
"child of God."

Tears and probably more tears will come before I get to see my son again. Tears of joy, knowing where he is, and tears of sadness because I cannot see him now and talk with him. But then there are tears of joy for what Christ did for us. We must remember to salute Him for this. Tears of joy are shed because we do not have to suffer in our sinfulness anymore.

Twenty-one-gun salutes go to Jesus our Savior, our King, our mighty soldier who came to defend us and win the victory for us that only He could win.

Soldier

Son
Obedient
Loyal
Dedicated
Individual
Establishing
Royalty

Oh Lord, as I lay my son to rest, I thank you. I thank you
for all the years you allowed me to know this fine person
we call my son. He was unique to say the least. Where he
got all his attributes, I do not know – well, yes, I do: They
came from you, Lord. As you look down upon us, Lord,
may we remember how he impacted all our lives? He
touched each one of us in a special and unique way. He
blessed us with his presence. He will be missed. Can you
ever replace someone? No. That is why, Lord, you sent the
Holy Spirit to come and comfort us until we see you and
our loved ones again. You are so good, Lord. You provide
our every need. Daily you bless us with sons and daughters
that each of us feels is the best in the world. We are so
blessed, Lord. We forget sometimes when we grumble and
complain about each other. Forgive us, Lord.
Keeping hate, revenge and terror going is not what you
want us to do.
If I can ask just one thing of you today when we lie my son
to rest, Lord, may we be more like Thee and less like
ourselves? May we selflessly put away things that are not
becoming to us and may we become united in the love you
shed for us?

Thank you, Lord, for the ultimate sacrifice that you made. Bless us once again.

Thank you for the sacrifice Christopher made for us. In Jesus, dear and precious name, I pray amen.

Thank You, Son

Thank you, son, thank you for going for me!
Thank you for your word to defend our country
And you are defending it!!!
Thank you, son, for standing with other soldiers who, just
like you,
have cares and concerns that they are leaving behind.
You are going to accomplish far more than you could think
or ask,
if God is your first choice.
In Him we live and breathe.
Thank you, son, for wearing your uniform so proudly.
Remember I love you so very much, and I am expecting
you home soon.
I am entrusting you to God.
Love you always,
MOM

The Appearance

With a friend, I went to have some special time
To talk about the hurt that was mine.
As we walked toward the place to eat,
I saw a person, but we did not speak.
I looked at him closely, not believing my eyes.
Could it be Christopher? It could not be denied!
He walked by me, I could almost touch.
But it couldn't be him! That would be too much!
After we were moments inside, I had to ask,
"Did you see what I saw?" That would be the task:
To believe someone pronounced dead
Is seen by my eyes alive instead!
Her answer was so quickly said,
"I wish you hadn't seen him," and our conversation was
led
To wonders of wondering if it was true.
Christopher, was that really you?
I ask myself years later, what was wrong with me?
Why didn't I ask him, "Who can you be?"
Others have said that is true.
They confessed they had seen you too.
Life can be a mystery why we are allowed
A bestowed humility, so we don't become proud.
God wants us to become as children
That is when we win.
I know that He cares for us
And in Him I must trust,
Leaving all things up to Him,
Just like it is and has always been.
Not knowing for sure if it was Chris or not.
At least I know that it was my lot

To see this person who looked like him,
Understanding that it might have been
A precious gift left for me.
Seeing my son just one more time!
The truth God has I will always find.
The truth of love we can always trust.
The reason to hope, the reason to live.

Bring All Your Sorrows

Bring all your sorrows,
All your disappointments,
I will bear them,
Carry them for you.

I weep,
I weep with you.
Cry, and I will wipe your tears.
I understand. I do, I do.

Let me hold you in my arms.
I stretch out my arms to you.
Will you turn away,
Or will you weep away my comfort?

Your tears are precious in my sight.
They are like diamonds.
They sparkle.
The tears will soon be your delight.

Pillars of Light

From the time that I heard about my son's death, the Lord gave me two songs: "Peace Like a River" and "Be Still My Soul" were going through my mind, allowing me the perfect peace that He promised in His word. He reassured me of His presence and made me feel like I was on wings of an eagle until after the service.

When I got home, I opened the curtains and saw pillars of light. There were pillars of light! The Lord said to me, "This birthday Chris will be with me." What peace! What marvelous peace He gave to me, and I am forever grateful for His mercy and grace.

I remembered that before Christopher was born, I dreamt that he was wrapped in a lime-green blanket. I believe he was wrapped in the love of the Lord for serving our country and the Lord.
How marvelous is His love for us?

The Curtains of Time

Pulling back the curtains of time,
Wondering, but nothing to find.

Seeking peace only God can give.
Looking for comfort to live.

What will tomorrow bring to me?
What could I possibly see?

Looking out the window,
What had come so low?

Not just one column of light to show,
But many more.

Your son will be with me.
This I want you to know.

These candles of light, like on a cake.
This birthday with me, your Father,
He will partake.

Christopher

Christopher, we love you
Christopher, we miss you
Thank you for being my son.
Thank you for serving and giving your life.
Thank you for the memories.

If you think my life was spaced,
Come to the graveyard I am there.
Quiet as each hour passes.
When will we be still at last?

The Pureness of Tears

Before my tears touched the ground, you touched me. You took a tear and covered me with it. The salt has not lost the savior.

Savoring the moment of a teardrop running down the face, cleansing the moment of deep sorrow only to have another tear chase it down the same cheek, impressing upon it its red streak, the Savior stands there with a bottle filled with His holy sorrows. This flowing balm will be poured onto a soul to redeem it from hatred or despair or failure to understand a rejection. Tears of salt are delicious only to the soul that has been redeemed.

The Lord touches the soul and heals the deep emptiness within, filling it with what is necessary to complete the adventure of life. It is a healing solution of forgiveness, understanding and self-acceptance. Jesus is the only source of such miraculous cure.

Because He loves you, He stands by and awaits your cries for Him. Because He loves you, He waits longer than anyone would be willing to wait to snatch your tear and mold it into a jewel of understanding and love. He will only leave if you say you do not want Him. But how could you tell someone who loves you so deeply to depart? He wants to wrap His loving arms around you so tightly that it will take your breath away, and He will breathe new life into your being.

When you cry Lord, deliver me from this pain that causes my eyes to leak.

The Master of Tears is the jeweler who sees the purity of your shimmering-diamond-tears in the rough. He converts them into a shedding of tenderness sometimes even from untender persons. In just a moment of time, the Master can break the barrier of a mean will built by hatred, fear, anger and disgust. This happens in that small moment when forgiveness and understanding flow in answer to cries for help. Not a drop is wasted. The bottle of forgiving, forgetting and joy is labeled and put in a special place for you to use whenever you need this treasure.

Therefore, treasure each moment of precious time. Everyone can cry, but not everyone can see the beauty in a tear. Most of us would rather hide the sad experiences and not share them with anyone. Remember, the Lord says He will never leave or forsake us. And He doesn't, and He will not, and we must not push that time away, as it is a tender moment for us to share with Him. Why bottle our emotions when the Lord's bottle of healing is in its special place for us?

The Lord wept. He understands the moments that only tears express.

A Day in November

November 29, 2006

This is my version of what it is like to be a soldier of
Jesus: A soldier for our country is very near and dear to
my heart. As you all may know, my son was taken to
heaven. He has been a blessing to me and I have heard
stories of his service. I did receive a letter that a soldier
had written to my son. It gave me great comfort. The
soldier called Christopher a "little shepherd." Christopher's
last name, Kleinwachter, means "little watchman."
The great Watchman came and got him.
I have heard that more soldiers are committing suicide then
are being killed in action. This is heartbreak!
My heart's desire is to reach out and leave no man or
woman behind.
Would you be willing to support me and assist in showing
what Jesus can mean to them?

About the Author

The Last Steps of Christopher was written mainly as a thank you to the military and the National Guard for what they did for me and my family. We can never repay all their efforts and love put to our family in laying Christopher to rest. The story of Christopher's death and the horrible pain it brought me now will be a source of healing for many. My book is my gift to others who have lost a loved one in serving our country in any way.

I am a small-town farm girl who played in sports and held the shotput title for many years after I graduated. I gave a half-hearted prayer to give God the glory for this. I followed in the footsteps of three sisters who also excelled in sports.

Being a red head and a having an extroverted personality presented me many challenges. I went to college for a short time to receive an Associate of Arts degree. Then I decided I would work for a while. I met my ex-husband at a wedding. We got married, had four children and then separated after 14 years of not-holy bliss. Despite many years of struggles, I kept my spirits up. On my jobs, I was awarded "Employee of the Month" three times, I became the top verifier at a telemarketing company, and I was nominated for the Hospitality Award of Grand Forks, North Dakota.

I would not be who I am today had it not been for the many hills and valleys of life. It is the facing of challenges that builds our character and strength.

www.ingramcontent.com/pod-product-compliance
Lightning Source LLC
LaVergne TN
LVHW010025070426
835509LV00001B/11